GOOD ENGLISH

how to speak it and to write it

David Arscott

POMEGRANATE · PRESS ·

Published by Pomegranate Press,
Church Cottage, Westmeston, Hassocks, Sussex BN6 8RH
Telephone/fax: 01273 846743
E-mail: 106461.1316@compuserve. com

David Arscott read English Language and Literature at
Hertford College, Oxford. A writer and broadcaster, he is
the author of more than twenty books, fiction and non-fiction.

British Library Cataloguing-in-Publication Data.
A catalogue record for this book is available from the British Library.

ISBN 0 9519876 3 1

Printed in England by M.D. Morgan, Red Lake Terrace, Ore,
Hastings, Sussex.

Saying what you mean

. . . and meaning what you say

Most of us, to the delight of our drooling grandparents, manage something quite like speech before we're two years old. By the age of five we not only have a vocabulary of several hundred words (some of which the doting old couple aren't quite so fond of), but display a surprising understanding of our complex, often illogical language. A great start - and yet vast numbers of adults are uneasily aware that they lack sufficient mastery of English either to express themselves well or to avoid making embarrassing mistakes.

Enter GOOD ENGLISH, which hacks away at the tangled thicket of confusions while never becoming a dull grammar lesson.

This, you'll be relieved to know, is *not* a guide to good manners, encouraging you to be always on your best linguistic behaviour. If you remember being taught not to split your 'infinitives' or to begin sentences with 'and', it will raise your spirits to know that such rules are now widely regarded as artificial - and if you *weren't* taught such things there's no point in worrying your pretty/handsome/strangely memorable head about them now.

And (couldn't resist it) this is certainly not a guide for purists, who will wish to qualify every statement with a thousand *yes, buts*. May, for example, *buts* be used in this way? (You bet!)

Although we don't flinch from including a smattering of simple grammar, with a few terms which may at first seem a little off-putting, GOOD ENGLISH is essentially an aid to clear thinking and confident self-expression.

We look at the way the language is put together; take you through punctuation and the dreaded apostrophe; highlight the most common mistakes; and, as a parting shot, offer you an entertaining exercise designed to show you just how much you've learned.

Trust us: it's far easier than you've been led to believe.

1

Great modern myths - no 1

"There's no such thing as Good English"

It was a pretty daring move to give the book this title, because there's a hit squad out there eager to rough up anyone who dares to promote a standard form of English. Our crimes include elitism and neo-colonialism.

The variety of English dialects spoken throughout the world is certainly good for the vitality of the language, but the anything-goes mafiosi forget that each of these regional forms has its own, often uncodified, 'rules and regulations'. Each, that is, has its accepted standard.

To encourage people to ignore the norms of their mother tongue is to betray those who most need a skilful use of language in order to feel socially at ease, to make themselves better understood or to get themselves a decent job - the very people, in short, for whom this book has been written.

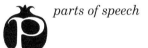

It can't be helped: if we're going to talk sensibly about our language, we'll have to agree on a few basic terms of reference. But don't worry - there aren't very many of them.

Nuts and bolts

We're vaguely aware that we speak, or write, in sentences - though just what *makes* a sentence is something we discuss elsewhere.

Let's take a sentence apart the way we'd strip down a car engine or dismantle the vacuum cleaner (and perhaps with a greater chance of putting it back together again).

For example: *Brave Gerald swiftly seized the beefy burglar.*

Sentences, as you may have noticed, are made up of words, and the words have separate functions. Stay with us for the no-frills, tourist class excursion.

NOUNS

'Things' to you and us - but not necessarily solid objects. In our example *Gerald* is a noun, and so is *burglar*. But Gerald might equally have grasped an idea, and then *idea* would have been a noun as well.

PRONOUNS

The humble understudies of such stage-strutting nouns as *Gerald* - familiar stand-ins for the real things, like *he*, *she*, *they* and *it*. If we'd already established that Gerald was a macho kind of guy, and if we'd already mentioned the burglar and his beefiness, we might have said: '*He* swiftly seized *him*' - two pronouns instead of two nouns.

A noun verbing another noun. But don't worry: you'll find reading through this book much lighter work.

3

VERBS

'Doing words' is the customary tag, though you don't have to be as aggressive as Gerald to qualify. He might have merely *contemplated* the burglar, or only *imagined* him: verbs both.

ADJECTIVES

This colourful lot are the 'describing words' - here *brave* and *beefy*. They 'qualify' the noun (that is, tell us something more about it), and they're so amazingly varied that you may not immediately recognise them for what they are: '*Well-intentioned* Gerald swiftly seized the *lone* burglar.'

ADVERBS

Just as adjectives quality nouns, so adverbs qualify verbs - they tell us something extra about the doing words. It's doubtful, come to think of it, that you could seize anyone gradually, but in this case we know that Gerald was headline news in the local newspaper because he acted *swiftly*.

Most adverbs end with *ly* but, as with adjectives, you may be deceived: 'He swam *fast* and *in a strenuous manner*, but drowned *horribly*.' Three adverbs, though the second is, properly, an 'adverbial phrase' - a cluster of words doing the same job as a single one.

Screws and washers . . . a few of the smaller bits

Even the humblest words have their technical names, and a few are worth remembering.

a, an are the 'indefinite articles' - because they're so airily vague.

'He ate *an* apple *a* day': any old apple on any old day.

the is 'the definite article' - bold, brash, no messing.

'He took a bite from *the* apple Griselda had chosen for him, and became violently ill': the particular apple he would never forget.

on, into, from, towards and a host of similar insignificant, but indispensable, little things are the 'prepositions' - marking the relation between two other words.

'Mind *over* matter'; 'travel *in* hope'; 'far *from* home'.

4

Sentencing policy

We speak them all the time without giving them a thought, but organising sentences on the page is another matter altogether . . .

Griselda drank.

That may not be a memorable statement, but we offer it to you as our first example of a sentence.

This is, to quote the Oxford English Dictionary (OED), 'a series of words in connected speech or writing, forming the grammatically complete expression of a single thought.'

We can, of course, add some words to our opener to make a more informative sentence, such as *Griselda drank the coffee* or, to reveal yet futher details of a mis-spent life, *Golden-curled Griselda noisily drank the instant decaffeinated coffee.*

What you'll have noticed (if you were concentrating) is that every time we complete a sentence we shut if off with a full stop, before starting a new one with a capital letter. That's the end of that.

You may also have noticed, with a shudder, that word 'grammatically' in the OED quote. A sentence usually has a subject (the noun that is doing the work or having the experience: in this case *Griselda*) and a verb (*drank*). It often also has an object (the noun that the verb acts upon: the *coffee*). And, as we've seen, it may carry extra baggage in the form of adverbs (*noisily*) and adjectives (*golden-curled, instant decaffeinated*).

We met these, in case you've already forgotten, on the previous page: they'll soon become old friends.

We could spread the info further while still keeping it within the bounds of a sentence: *Golden-curled Griselda noisily drank the instant decaffeinated coffee which her* mother had bought the day before in a branch of Tesco while on a visit to her aged aunt in Pinner.

That, despite all the extra bits, is the 'expression of a single thought': it's telling us, if tediously, that Griselda drank coffee. End of idea. If we wish to add that it burned her tongue we're entering new mental territory - and we need a new sentence.

Here's how Ernest Hemingway would have done it: *Griselda drank the coffee. It burned her tongue. Cojones! You couldn't even trust the damned coffee.*

Manly staccato stuff. One short sentence following another. Subject, verb, object, full stop. Sometimes just a single word. Life is tough, hombre.

If, however, you'd like a little more flow in your composition, you might decide to link some of your sentences together. There's one legitimate way of doing this, and another that must be

RIGHT

> Gerald caught a burglar. He was rewarded.
>
> or
>
> Gerald caught a burglar, and he was rewarded.
>
> not
>
> Gerald caught a burglar, he was rewarded.

WRONG

avoided like the plague.

First, the approved method. You hitch the sentences together with a handy coupling device which has the nasty and offputting name <u>conjunction</u> but which is immediately familiar in the guise of words such as *and* or *but*. So: *Griselda drank the coffee and / but / although / because* (strange creature) *it burned her tongue.*

One sentence now has two built into it, and it's not difficult to fit a third - even a fourth - in there, too: *Griselda drank the coffee <u>and</u> it burned her tongue, <u>but</u> she still managed a wan smile <u>because</u> she was a game sort of girl.*

Making paragraphs

Sentences can stand alone, but they have a habit of clustering into paragraphs - which raises the sticky question of where to break off one paragraph and start another.

There is no hard and fast rule about this, but you should think about starting a new paragraph whenever there's a change of mood or if you begin to develop a new train of thought.

The best bet for beginners is to look closely at how the professionals do it. But don't turn to the popular newspapers for guidance: sub editors like plenty of white space, and (especially in the tabloids) will often make a series of short sentences into separate paragraphs merely for the sake of a quick read.

There comes a point at which the string becomes so entangled as to trip you up, but there's nothing at all wrong with our last exhibit from a purely grammatical point of view.

Now to what you must NOT do. The comma is a heavily worked device which represents a slight pause. It NEVER has the force of a full stop, and should never be used as one:

Thank you for catching that burglar, who else would have been so brave!

The objection to his kind of sloppiness isn't only that it breaks the rules, as it (horribly) does, but that it erects a barrier to understanding.

Any literate reader will attempt to run on the sense after *burglar*, perhaps for a moment imagining (God forbid) that it is the villain who is being praised for bravery rather than good old Gerald.

A few notable opening sentences in English literature . . .

'It was a bright cold day in April, and the clocks were striking thirteen.' (George Orwell: *Nineteen Eighty-Four*)

'Last night I dreamt I went to Manderley again.' (Daphne du Maurier: *Rebecca*)

'It was the afternoon of my eighty-first birthday, and I was in bed with my catamite when Ali announced that the archbishop had come to see me.' (Anthony Burgess: *Earthly Powers*)

'Lolita, light of my life, fire of my loins.' (Vladimir Nabokov: *Lolita*)

'It is a truth universally acknowledged, that a single man in possession of a good fortune must be in want of a wife.' (Jane Austen: *Pride and Prejudice*)

'Stately, plump Buck Mulligan came from the stairhead, bearing a bowl of lather on which a mirror and a razor lay crossed.' (James Joyce: *Ulysses*)

Alice was beginning to get very tired of sitting by her sister on the bank, and of having nothing to do: once or twice she had peeped into the book her sister was reading, but it had no pictures or conversations in it, and what is the use of a book,' thought Alice, 'without pictures or conversations?' (Lewis Carroll: *Alice's Adventures in Wonderland*)

Great modern myths - no 2

"Learning grammar stifles creativity"

Another classic piece of nonsense. What kind of performance would you expect from a naturally gifted footballer who refused to train, or a dancer who never exercised? Or how do you fancy going under the knife of a gung-ho surgeon who can't wait to slice those nasty lumpy things from your stomach lining, but has never bothered to find out how all the colourful bits inside join together?

A generation of children has been coached by enthusiastic English teachers eager to encourage free expression ('write about the feel of the sun beating on your face') without giving their little charges the means of communicating the experience to anyone else.

Just think of the writers you most enjoy, and ask yourself whether a good grounding in English got in the way of their creativity. Then imagine their books littered with weird punctuation and mis-spellings. Would you still read them?

 *punctuation*

. , : ; - ( ) " " ? !

So we all know what a full stop is for, and most of us (alas) feel pretty confident about sprinkling commas left, right and centre.

The fact is, however, that it's easy to make a nasty mess of punctuation - the little marks that can help your words dance and sing rather than stiffly galumph.

A mastery of them gives you the ringmaster's role: now slowing, now quickening the pace; sending in the clowns or the roaring lions; starting up the band, or - as the mood takes you - producing suspense, surprise, sensation.

Here, then, is a swift guide to the tools at your disposal. We begin with a familiar warning : until you've really got the hang of the rules, keep things simple. Full stops and a restrained use of commas will be quite enough to be going along with.

Dots & dashes

COMMA [,]

Did we suggest that commas were easy to use? Not so. They tend to be thrown into sentences at all sorts of odd places. Use them:

- in a list: *The sandwiches were filled with egg, ham, spinach and cucumber.* (No comma before the *and*).

- as brackets: *My uncle, who has one leg, plays golf brilliantly.* (You always need two. Commas, that is).

- after an introductory phrase: *Having arrested the burglar, Gerald was bursting with ill-stifled pride.*

- to avoid confusion: *Mary was in love with John, and Joe with Mary.* We should, perhaps, insert a comma here in any case, to suggest the pause we might hear if the sentence were spoken aloud, but the mark prevents our mistakingly believing that Mary loved both John and Joe.

9

punctuation

Commas in the wrong places are likely to cause confusion or hilarity:
Guests, who must leave before the end of the conference, should check out of the hotel at lunchtime.

The suggestion here is that all the guests are obliged to pack their bags early. The material between brackets (and between commas when they're being used used as brackets) should be removable without any loss to the sense. What we're left with here is: *Guests should check out of the hotel at lunchtime.* In fact, there's no need for commas at all in our original sentence.

COLON [:]

The 'wait for it!' punctuation mark:
The trees produced a bountiful harvest: nuts, apples and peaches.
There's no universal agreement about whether the first word after a colon should have a capital letter - unless, of course, it normally has a claim to one. We go for the feel of the thing, and would certainly (and with some satisfaction) write:
Here's my considered reply: Nuts!

Hold your breath for Henry James . . .

The novelist Henry James wrote some of the most labyrinthine sentences in our literature, and he needed a deft control of punctuation to see himself (and us) safely home. We don't recommend a similar prolixity when you send off your next job application or tap the bank manager for a loan, but this typical example from the master is well worth studying all the same:

Not yet so much as this morning had she felt herself sink into possession: gratefully glad that the warmth of the southern summer was still in the high, florid rooms, palatial chambers where hard, cool pavements took reflections in their lifelong polish, and where the sun on the stirred sea-water, flickering up through open windows, played over the painted 'subjects' in the splendid ceilings - medallions of purple and brown, of brave old melancholy colour, medals as of old reddened gold, embossed and beribboned, all toned with time and all flourished and scolloped and gilded about, set in their great moulded and figured concavity (a nest of white cherubs, friendly creatures of the air), and appreciated by the aid of that second tier of smaller lights, straight openings to the front, which did everything, even with the Baedekers and photographs of Milly's party dreadfully meeting the eye, to make of the place an apartment of state.

The Wings of the Dove

SEMICOLON [;]

So few people know how to use it that the semicolon has almost disappeared. It is, however, just the job for linking mini-sentences together in a list form, especially after a preceding colon: *The Government will fall for several reasons: it is incompetent; it contains the most unscrupulous set of rogues ever to disgrace the House; it has a majority of only three; and it has, understandably, lost its collective nerve.* Phew! Unlike commas in a list, the semi-colon is required to make a final showing before the *and*.

DASH [-]

A pair of dashes is rather more zestful than commas or brackets: *My father - a game old bird - will be arriving tomorrow.* But DON'T change your mind half way through: *My father - a game old bird, will...* A single dash, on the other hand, can be used for final emphasis - like this.

BRACKETS [( )]

Can also be overdone, but very useful for packing in information: *Apart from the reserve itself, with its well-marked nature trail (look out for the teasels used by cloth manufacturers to give their fabric a fluffy appearance), you can enjoy live exhibits (beetles and fish) in*

Hitching-to-the-waggon

The use of hyphens causes a great deal of perplexity, and we're sorry to tell you that there are no fixed rules. When a verb is 'qualified' by a noun or an adjective it's usual to insert one (reed-choked, strong-running), but windblown seems fine as a single word. Verbs qualified by an adverb (mightily pleased) are usually excused a hyphen, unless clarity demands one.

Use them sparingly, but be aware that they sometimes help to avoid confusion: a black cab driver may be a West Indian taxi driver or any old driver of a black London cab. If we mean the former we're probably wise to write black cab-driver even if that's not our normal usage; if the latter, black-cab.

---

the 18th century mill house. Note the commas: the usual rules apply.

SPEECH MARKS [" " ' ']

Single quotes are favoured today, as less messy: *'Sorry about your lip, Griselda,' he said.* But use the double variety when you need quotes within quotes: *'I'm never convinced when you say "Sorry", Gerald,' she replied.*

QUESTION MARK [?]

Use it only after a direct question (*'Who are you?'*), and not in reported speech: *She asked him who he was.*

EXCLAMATION MARK [!]

Hardly ever use it. Where there really is an exclamation (*Wow!*), fine. Otherwise your use of words should make any emphasis clear.

Dear Mr Carruthers,

I was most gratified to receive the Reward for catching the Burglar, and feel the Honour most deeply. Please thank your Sub Committee for the Letter

Capital punishment

Some folk like to be on their Very Best Behaviour when they write - and for many of them that means 'capping up' initial letters like fury. Or Fury.

Don't do it! Common practice today is to use lower case (small) letters as often as possible.

The Queen is our particular monarch and the Government is the one we elected, but otherwise kings and queens, governments and county councils, doctors and vicars, apples and pears, horses for courses.

 *the apostrophe*

Sins of omission - and possession

One little mark: so much confusion. The misplaced apostrophe (say it 'a-POS-tro-fee' if you really can't keep it out of the conversation) is spreading through the written universe like a mutant plant, threatening to invade and choke every word that contains a vulnerable final 's', regardless of sense.

Yes, folks, the humble apostrophe wins our coveted GOOD ENGLISH bad headache award.
 But help is at hand: keep taking the tablet on the next page and the pain will go away.

Before we explain the two principal uses of the apostrophe, let's mention a minor one: you'll often find it inserted where there are figures or numbers which might otherwise confuse.

Plural politicians and police constables sometimes appear as MP's and PC's, and some of us look back with fondness to the 1960's. Current practice is to dispense with the apostrophe in these cases (MPs, PCs, 1960s), but where lower case (rather than capital) letters are used it retains its value: *p's and q's.*

The apostrophe's two major uses are to indicate *1.* the omission of a letter or letters, and *2.* possession. What it is NEVER used for is to signal a plain plural: one chair, two chairs; one banana, two bananas; one tomato, two tomatoes; one choc, a box of chocs. *No apostrophe!*

1. Omission
Words such as *don't, let's, you'll* carry an apostrophe to show that something is missing from what would otherwise be *do not, let us* and *you will.*

Note that *there's* means *there is,* and should therefore NEVER be used with a plural, as in *There's loads of prizes to be won!* (There *are* loads, of course - and the best of luck to you.)

Note especially, and keep on noting, that the apostrophe in *it's* signals omission: *it is* (or *it has*).

It's NEVER signals possession. Keep saying to yourself *It's means it is; it's means it is; it's means it is* - and then, as madness beckons, turn the page . . .

13

2. Possession

This is the most common usage of all, but for some reason it sets the heads of otherwise mentally well-organised souls in a terrible spin.

The simple rule is to place your apostrophe-s ['s] after the person or thing that has the ownership. So: *Gerald's reward, the dog's dinner, the ship's prow.*

You'll notice that these are all in the singular (one Gerald/one reward; one dog/one dinner; one ship/one prow). This is difficult enough for many people, but the plurals tend to cause even more problems.

Rule a: If the owner is in the singular, it doesn't matter how many things he/she/it possesses - the *'s* remains just where you would expect it to be: *Griselda's injuries, Gerald's admirers, the dog's biscuits, the ship's funnels.*

Rule b: If the owner has the usual English plural ending of s, put your apostrophe *after* it - again, no matter whether the 'possessions' are singular or plural: *the ladies' room, the ladies' hats, the (several) dogs' owner, the dogs' kennels.* Note that you don't need an extra s here.

Rule c: If the plural is one of those oddities without an s ending (*men, children* etc), put an *apostrophe-s* after it: *men's, women's, children's.* Remember: the apostrophe always follows the plural form.

Rule d: Personal pronouns (his, hers, ours, yours, theirs etc) have no apostrophe at all: *John's* book used to be *hers.*

Unfortunately this rule extends to possessive *its,* which causes the biggest headache of the lot: *John's* book, which used to be *hers* and will one day be *theirs,* has lost *its* cover.

The tablet

(to be taken daily while symptoms persist)

It's always means it is/has.
(It's a fine day; it's mine; it's been so easy to learn)

Its is always used to signify possession.
(The dog wagged its tail; the story reached its end; its simplicity is beyond belief)

personal pronouns as subject and object

You, me and I

You and me: you and I. Which is right?

... as the song almost had it. Here's another danger area which can easily be avoided

If you ask the question in the belief that a single answer will meet every situation, you clearly need to read on. But don't worry. There's a simple test you can use every time, and you'll find that it won't let you down.

First, examine our *Exhibit A* at the foot of the page. Do you happen to spot anything wrong with those sentences?

Yes, of course you do. Dialect speakers may recognise some of those forms, which are therefore fitting where dialect is spoken, but anyone else knows, without a second thought, that by the norms of Standard English every single one of them is (comically) wrong.

You may feel that you don't need to know why they're off the wall, but please forgive us if we tell you.

There are two forms (subject and object) for most of the personal pronouns - one for when someone is leading the action (*she* drank the coffee) and another for when someone is acted upon (it burned *her*).

These subject/object pairings are well known to us all: *I / me, he / him, she / her, we / us, they / them, who / whom.* (*You* serves for both).

Now the good news: the hard work is nearly over.

So soon? Yes, the trick you use when in doubt is to rely on your knowledge of which half of the pair is right if used by itself - then simply add the details of anyone else involved.

Exhibit A

Me went to the dance.
Griselda complained bitterly to I.
Us like plum pudding.
The drinks are on we!
Him laughed like a drain.
I saw she riding a bike.
Them live next door.
We'll invite they to supper.

15

If it's *I went to the dance* (as of course it is), it's *You and I went to the dance*. If it's *Griselda complained bitterly to me*, it's *Griselda complained bitterly to you and me*.

Exhibit B gives the complete check list: if any of these sounds wrong to you, try to find some other way of expressing yourself.

Are there exceptions to the rule? In purely grammatical terms, No, though it would invite ridicule (unless you move in cucumber sandwich circles) to

reply *It is I* when asked 'Who's there?' *It's me*, though wrong, is right.

Beware the danger of saying something like *They gave generously*

to *we carol-singers* (which suggests that a choir of midgets is doing the rounds).

And please NEVER, EVER say *Between you and I.*

Exhibit B

You and I went to the dance.
Griselda complained bitterly to you and me.
We and the gang like plum pudding.
The drinks are on Sam and us.
He and I laughed like a drain.
I saw her and Jack riding a bike.
They and I live next door.
We'll invite you and them to supper.

. . . not to speak of Myself

We've noticed a creeping use of 'myself' by people who seem to think that 'Mary and I went to the dance' is rather snooty - just as others find 'He'll visit you and me' too low-brow.

Use it as an <u>intensifier</u> ('I don't eat bacon *myself*, though I buy it for my children') or <u>reflexively</u> ('I've burned *myself* with the damn coffee yet again'), but avoid the likes of 'Darren, Lulu and myself went to the disco.'

'Yourself went, eh?' is the proper response to that sort of clumsiness.

Here's another little problem that you know how to solve already...

Just a few minor rules:

- *Either* and *neither* are singular when only two people or things are involved (*'either/neither of them is acceptable'*), but in *neither/nor* the verb agrees with the subject nearest to it: *Neither he nor they drink coffee.*
- *Every, everyone, everybody, nobody* and *someone* are singular: *Every man and woman is here.*
- *Each* is singular (*Each guest burns her mouth*), except where the subject is plural (*The women each burn their mouths*).
- *Collective nouns* can be singular or plural according to taste, but don't change your mind in mid-sentence: *The family are taking its holiday abroad;* or *the Government is adamant about their policy.*
OUCH!

Having to agree

No marks at all for spotting what's wrong with this sentence: *The bus were late.*

Or with this one: *We was cross.*

And even if you have to pause for a moment before explaining why they both offend, you'll quickly agree with us when we say that a <u>singular</u> *bus* demands a *was*, and that a <u>plural</u> *we* should have a *were*.

A subject, to put it in grammatical (but extremely simple) language, must 'agree' with its verb. If one is singular, so must the other be; and, likewise, a plural noun requires a plural verb.

If this is so obvious, why does it so often go wrong? Pure carelessness!

Consider the following examples:

The glory of this football club are the cups and medals in its display cabinet.

A flotilla of ships were sailing into port.

Griselda, along with a few of her friends, are holding a coffee tasting today.

All are wrong, and each requires only a little thought. The glory (singular) *is*, no matter how many trophies the club may boast. The flotilla, similarly, *was* sailing, however vast. And Griselda *is*, perhaps unwisely, about to drink more coffee: her friends are put between commas (effectively brackets) and the plural verb would be correct only in *Griselda and a few of her friends are holding a party.* In that case the phrase *Griselda and a few of her friends* becomes the subject of the verb.

See our panel on the left for more enthralling details.

17

Great modern myths - no 3

"Anything goes as long as they understand you"

This is the routine excuse for slipshod English, and it's fatally flawed even by its own careless standards. The sorry fact is that anyone unable to control the language is all too likely to be very badly misunderstood indeed.

Even if they catch your drift well enough, however, the people you inflict with your errors aren't likely to be hugely impressed - and, unfair though it may be, they're likely to make cruel and sweeping judgements about your intelligence.

It's hardest to accept this shoulder-shrugging myth when it's parroted by those who should know better: people who can handle English perfectly well themselves. It may be gratifying to know that they're tolerant of your mistakes. The sad fact is that they'll have a similarly relaxed attitude towards your varicose veins and that persistent, inoperable pain in your gut.

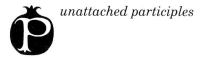

unattached participles

*Pssst!
This one can
make you look
pretty stupid*

Hanging around

. . . waiting for an accident to happen

Being soft as a jelly, I sent the boiled egg back to the kitchens.

If that sentence doesn't make you snigger, then either *a.* you haven't got a sense of humour or *b.* you're not yet attuned to the pitfalls of what is variously called the hanging, dangling, wandering or unattached participle.

Bear with us while we explain that a <u>present participle</u> is the part of a verb ending in *-ing* which often acts as an adjective: *playing* card, *washing* powder, *walking* boots. It very often, as above, begins an <u>adjectival phrase</u> (a cluster of words such as *Being soft as a jelly*).

The other thing to know about this present participle is that, like all adjectives, it lusts after a noun to latch on to - and that (you'll have met the type) it fastens upon the very first one that it meets.

Now we can see what's wrong with the example above. Perhaps the writer meant us to understand that the egg was soft, but the first

noun that the *Being* phrase meets is *I*. What he is actually telling us, therefore, is that he himself was soft as a jelly. He had better try again: *Because the boiled egg....*

This is such a common mistake that, once your eye is in, you'll find it practically everywhere:

While agreeing with the Government's overall policy, will the Prime Minister not . . . (It would be strange, surely, if the PM failed to agree with his own policy.)

Stopping suddenly in front of the picture, his glasses fell off. (What made the spectacles assume a life of their own?)

Having studied your letter with interest, the cattle should probably be sold at auction. (Quadrupeds with such abilities should fetch a very high price indeed.)

But it isn't only *-ing* phrases that are involved in these weird scenarios. Any adjectival phrase is likely to be caught up in the action.

unattached participles

Burned to the ground during the Civil War, the present house was rebuilt in 1850. (A failure of logic here: it obviously wasn't the present house that was burned down).

Squat, yellow, hairy and giving off a repulsive odour, I replaced the exotic fruit on the shelf with a shudder. (Ah, yes, the shudder was well deserved).

Wearing an odd assortment of hats, he assumed that they were on their way to a fancy dress party.

Only nearly wrong

The positioning of individual words can lead to misunderstanding or absurdity, the worst offenders being _only_ and _nearly_. Consider:

I've only been sitting in the office for an hour.
  (Shouldn't you have been doing some work, too? Or did you mean to say: *I've been sitting in the office for only an hour*?)

We nearly walked as far as the seafront.
  (But you decided to take the bus after all? Or do you mean: *We walked nearly as far as the seafront*?)

It's obviously impossible to avoid this kind of thing in everyday conversation, but do look out for it in your written English.

You're familiar with the agony: a choice has to be made between two words, and you know that the wrong move will show you up as an ignoramus. Here's help . . .

Fewer mistakes, less confusion

Fewer/less is easy to get right once you understand that *fewer* is used only for number and *less* for quantity. Griselda, therefore, couldn't drink *fewer* coffee, however hard she tried, but she could certainly drink *fewer coffees* (or *less coffee*). Similarly, she couldn't apply *less* plasters to her lips, but *less plaster* (a smaller amount of the stuff) or *fewer plasters* would improve her looks no end.

Supermarkets, with their 'Five items or less' signs, have been among the worst offenders, but seem to be improving.

Lay/lie. Hens *lay* eggs when they *lie* on the straw, and they are still *laying* them when they are *lying* on the straw. The trouble is that they also *laid* eggs yesterday when they *lay* (hence, not to say hens, the ghastly confusion) on the straw.

Yes, it's the fact that the present tense of *lay* mimics the past tense of *lie* that causes most of the problems.

May/might. A source of difficulty similar to the above, in that *might* is not only the past tense of *may* (I think I *may* do it; I thought I *might* do it), but has its own subtly different present tense meaning, too.

I *may* do it leaves the question open (it's entirely possible, but I simply don't know); whereas I *might* do it suggests a more remote possibility. Yes, it could happen, but I'm not really thinking about doing it just yet: *pigs might fly* first.

Since the nuances of this pairing could fill several pages, we'll content ourselves with one last comparison:

I may have done it (it's possible, but I don't know or can't remember.)

I might have done it (but, as it happens, I didn't.)

Shall/will. Another minefield, the most simple rule being that I and we *shall*; he, she, it, you and they *will*. If you wish to be emphatic, however, the opposite applies:

'You *shall* go to the ball, Cinders'; 'I *will* have my way.'

None is/none are. When you mean <u>not one is</u> use the former: *none of us is perfect.*

When you mean that no people or things are, use the latter: *there are none left.*

H.W. Fowler, the language guru, stated that *number* should be regarded as

---

A (light) touch of the verbals

Since we've begun to talk about past and present tenses of verbs, it's obviously high time that we tackled a subject that's apt to put the fear of God into otherwise brave and indomitable folk. In true GOOD ENGLISH fashion, however, we shan't get involved in the kind of details that are of no use to you - and we're confident that you'll very soon wonder what all the fuss was about.

Young children soon master the spoken language because it follows rules that their brains understand at an unconscious level. When it comes to verbs, they learn the common-or-garden pattern *I play/ I played; I cry/I cried; I chase/I chased.* These are called <u>regular</u> verbs, because they all behave in the same convenient way.

Our tiny tots, however, are equally likely to say *I see/I seed*, imagining the English language to be a logical thing - which, of course, it isn't. The verb *to see* is one of many <u>irregular</u> verbs, which we can learn only from experience.

Now we've got that out of the way we're going to give you a list of the main tenses, using the regular verb *to munch* (why not?) as a model.

As usual, you'll just have to shrug your shoulders about some of the names. We do need labels to describe what we're talking about, after all. Be tolerant.

Infinitive: *To munch.*
Simple present tense: *I munch.*
Continuous present: *I am munching.*
Future: *I shall munch.*
Simple past: *I munched.*
Past imperfect: *I was munching.*
Past perfect: *I have munched.*
Imperative: *Munch!*
Conditional mood: *I would/should be munching.*
Subjunctive mood (for hypothetical situations): *(If) I were munching.*

You can drive yourself crazy with the likes of *I shall have been munching* - but enough is as good as a feast.

singular with the definite article (*the number of entrants was* small) and plural with an indefinite article (*only a small number have* entered).

Which / that. Compare: *The reward, which amounted to a cool thousand pounds, meant less to Gerald than the adulation,* with *This is the cup of coffee that scalded poor Griselda's lips.*

In the first example, *which* gives us some information we didn't have, whereas *that* in the second simply defines the particular cup involved.

The two are, however, increasingly regarded as being interchangeable.

Who / whom / whose. We use *whom* rarely today, as it sounds affected, but there are those occasions when nothing else will do. *Who* and *whom* are the subject and object of the pronoun (like *I*

and *me*). So: *Who is coming to the party?* (I am.) *For whom is the party being given?* (For me, lucky dog.) *And who is going with whom?* (That'd be telling.)

Note, in passing, *who's / whose*, as in *We don't know who's* (who is) *going to end up crying on whose* (pronoun) *shoulder.*

It's a brave soul who can say *For whom are you waiting?* (correct), rather than (incorrect) *Who are you waiting for?* and we wouldn't recommend it in the real, heartless world.

Sometimes you just gotta be street-wise!

Not likely . . .

The word <u>like</u> has many uses (*we were like-minded; I like black coffee; your face is like a melon*), but it should NOT be used when you mean either 'such as', 'as' or 'as if'.

Ball games <u>like</u> hockey and cricket are not allowed in the park suggests that only games bearing a resemblance to those two are forbidden (so that you might, in all innocence, arrange a game of American football), whereas *Ball games <u>such as</u> hockey and cricket are not allowed* uses those sports merely as examples of ball games the authorities don't like.

Not: *She cried <u>like</u> never before,* but *She cried <u>as</u> never before.*

Not: *He ran <u>like</u> he would never stop,* but *He ran <u>as if</u> he would never stop.*

Commonly erred

Excuse the awful pun, but the fact is that you can usually get away with something as dreadful as that (despite the howls) if it's intentional. Unconscious misuses of the language, on the other hand, are more often suffered in grim silence. Here are a few of the regulars . . .

The reason is because. Logic will (or should) tell you that the reason for something can't be caused by anything else: *The reason for Griselda's anger was <u>that</u> Gerald failed to notice her wounds.*

Try and. This, for some reason, seems to be replacing 'try to', which is obviously the correct usage: *Gerald said that he would try <u>to</u> get home, but had an important golf match to play.*

Centred around. Another failure of logic: *The inflammation was centred <u>on</u> her upper lip, the shape of which had once so excited him.*

Didn't use to. The negative of 'use to' is always getting mangled: *Gerald and Griselda used to be such lovebirds. They <u>used not</u> to quarrel at all.*

Those kind of thing. 'Those' is plural and 'kind' is singular, so they simply don't match: *Griselda used to complain that <u>those kinds</u> of kettle failed to bring water to the boil, but <u>this kind</u> of remark never passes her sadly swollen lips these days.*

Run quicker/slower. A common mistake. 'Quicker' and 'slower' are adjectives *(The <u>slower</u> tortoise nevertheless won the race)* and the matching adverbs are 'quickly' and 'slowly': *She ran <u>quickly</u> for the first aid box, while he ran <u>more quickly</u> in the opposite direction.*

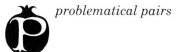

problematical pairs

Our market research tells us that many readers have difficulty with these pairs - and we trust that our brief guide pares the errors from their English.

Double trouble

Affect/effect. To *affect* something is to influence it, as in *Sending on the substitute affected the course of the match.* To *effect*, on the other hand, is to bring something about: *The directors effected the change from building society to limited company so deftly that nobody complained.*

The noun is *effect*, as in: *His schooling with the Jesuits had a marked effect on him.*

Uninterested/disinterested. A bored schoolboy is *uninterested.* A judge or referee, however fascinating they happen to find their work, should be *disinterested* - impartial, with no personal interest, financial or otherwise, in the result.

Imply/infer. These two are NOT interchangeable. To *imply* is to suggest: *Gerald implied that Griselda was rather stupid not to notice how hot the coffee was.* To *infer* is to deduce or conclude: *The evidence led Gerald to infer that the apple had been tampered with.*

Practice/practise. Noun/verb: *Make it your practice to practise the correct use of English.*

Licence/license. Noun/verb: *He obtained a licence/the magistrates licensed him to be the licensee.*

Advice/advise. Noun/verb: *Take my advice, and never advise a learner to jump in at the deep end.*

Past/passed. Past can be a noun (*archaeologists make a study of the past*), an adjective (*he is one of our past presidents*), an adverb (*the cars swept past*) or a preposition (*it's half past six*). BUT *passed* is always a verb (in the past tense): *He passed the ball/she passed him the apple with a malevolent smile/the time for talking had surely passed.*

Brought/bought. Dangerously similar, these are the past tenses of *bring/buy*: *She brought me the bag she had bought for a fiver.*

Continual/continuous. A *continual* action is repeated over and over, whereas something continuous is uninterrupted: *He continually came to the meetings, his support for our cause being continuous through thick and thin.*

25

Dependant/dependent. Noun and adjective. A dependant is someone who relies on someone else for support, whereas dependent means 'hanging down' or 'relying (upon)'.

Principal/principle. A *principal* (noun) is a head man or woman, giving us the adjective *principal*, meaning 'main, chief, first in rank'. A principle is a fundamental law or a general rule, commonly used to imply a moral standard, as in: *Our principal was a woman of principle.*

Definite/definitive. Something which is *definite* is unmistakably clear, whereas *definitive* means 'final, authoritative': *After hearing the court's definitive judgement of our case, we decided to draw up a definite plan of action.*

Depreciate/deprecate. To *depreciate* is to fall in value, but to *deprecate* is to express disapproval: *Griselda deprecated the fact that her new car depreciated by a thousand pounds when Gerald, suffering severe stomach pains, drove it into a tree.*

Lo(a)th/Loathe. *Grisdelda was lo(a)th* (unwilling) *to tell Gerald that she had begun to loathe him.*

Practical/practicable. Practical is the opposite of theoretical, whereas *practicable* means 'feasible, capable of being carried out: *A supremely practical man, he could mend almost anything you gave him, but he would never take on a job that he knew wasn't practicable.*

Fortuitous/fortunate. The former means 'happening by accident' - and not necessarily for the better: *It was fortuitous that the cliff should crumble at the very moment that he began to climb it, and very fortunate for him that he managed to escape with his life.*

Lose/loose. Simple, really: *When Griselda asked Gerald kindly not to lose his temper, he looked at her as if she had a screw loose.*

Refute/deny. No, they don't look the same, but (as with imply/infer) one half of the pair is often wrongly used. To *refute* does NOT mean 'to claim that something isn't true' (which is, of course, to *deny* it), but to prove it false. This is, you will hardly deny, quite another matter. A supposedly impartial BBC news reporter who says: *The Chancellor today refuted claims that his budget was unfair to pensioners* is actually telling us that the Government is right (having disproved its critics' assertions) and that the pensioners are, indeed, getting a fair deal.

Is that what he meant to say?

spelling

The *(startling)* fact that university students have asked us for clarification of to/two/too (as in *To take two sweets is too greedy*); here/hear (as in *Stand here and you'll hear the nightingales sing*); and they're/their/there (as in *They're pleased that their car is over there*), suggests that long inattention to spelling has left many of them cruelly handicapped in a world which still demands basic standards of literacy.

If you have a spelling hang-up, our advice is to carry a dictionary with you at all times. As a short-cut, however, here's the GOOD ENGLISH primer of the most commonly mis-spelt words - these, natch, being the correct versions.

And don't feel stupid about your blind spots: we all have them.

i before *e* (thief, grief) except after *c* (receive)

Well, that's what they taught us at school. But beware of some *weird* exceptions.

Spell-checking

Our Top 100

abhorrent
abysmal
accommodation
accumulate
acknowledge
acquaintance
acquire
advice *(noun)*
advise *(verb)*
aerial
affect (influence)
aisle (church)
ambulance
aquarium
attendant
beginning
believe
changeable
chaos
chronological
commission
committee
conceive
conceptual

consensus
courteous
crystal
currant (fruit)
current (now)
deceive
defer/deferred
dependant (person)
dependent (reliant)
desperate
disappeared
effect (bring about)
elementary
embarrass
equivalent
exercise
fulfil/fulfilment
fulfilling
gaseous
gauge
gradually
harass
hassle
hirsute
incessant
independent
infer/inferred
instalment
island/isle
knowledge
licence *(noun)*
license *(verb)*
livelihood
lovable/loveable
maintenance
malleable
millennium
miscellaneous

monstrous
movable/moveable
murmur
necessary
negotiate
occasionally
occur/occurred
offer/offered
omission/omit
partial
practice *(noun)*
practise *(verb)*
precede/precedent
predecessor
prefer/preferred
prevalent/ence
principal (chief)
principle (rule)
privilege
proceed
receive
recession
refer/referred
relevant/relevance
relief
repellant *(noun)*
repellent *(adj)*
separate
skilful
stationary (still)
stationery (paper)
supercilious
superintendent
supersede
tomorrow
unmistakable
unnecessary
virtuous

Meet the strange little ghoti

No, not an aquarian exotic. Say it:
gh as in *enough*
o as in *women*
ti as in *motion*
Ain't English daft!

Great modern myths - no 4

"Language evolves, so any change is OK"

A familiar defence of bad English, whose advocates have the smug feeling that history is on their side. But ask them about something that matters to them (sport, the arts, the countryside) and they'll very soon tell you that change isn't always for the better.

No, we can't stem the tide, but that shouldn't blind us to unfortunate abuses of the language - particularly where its clarity is affected.

To lose the word 'disinterested' because of its steady merging with 'uninterested' [see page 25] may be inevitable but, if so, it will be yet another small, but real, impoverishment of our ability to communicate effectively with one another.

Its precision is one of the glories of the English language. Be vigilant!

 *the test*

Write on one side of the paper only

Our book wouldn't be respectable without an 'exam', would it? We reckon there are 40 mistakes in this story. How many can you spot?

line

1   'Between you and I,' said Griselda, as her friends arrived for coffee, 'Gerald
2   rather resents the childrens' success. Its effected him badly.'
3   It was a fine, spring morning, the garden was at it's brilliant best.
4   'Wayne, Tara and myself went to the music festival,' she explained, 'but
5   he was too disinterested to come. He said he had to practice his golf swing.'
6   She had just noticed that there were less cups than visitors, when
7   Gerald walked in. He was carrying a golf club - a niblick, and he looked
8   angry.
9   'I heard you infer that I don't care about the kids,' he said. 'I refute that.'
10   Having started her story, the climax of it was something Griselda didn't
11   intend to leave out.
12   'I may not have seized a beefy burglar,' she continued pointedly, 'but the
13   rest of the family managed to enhance its reputation with there singing. I
14   sometimes wonder if that matters to you?'
15   'I would of thought,' Gerald countered, 'that my needs were greater than
16   their's. For who do you make the effort? The children. Their the principle
17   thing in your life. Try and see things from my point of view for a change.'
18   'We nearly won all the cups,' Griselda persisted starting to pour the
19   coffee. 'Everyone were very impressed. We may have won them all if
20   Prunella hadn't caught a cold. She wouldn't take my advise, but went out
21   in the rain.'
22   'Poor lamb,' Gerald snarled, striding passed her. 'Enjoy you're coffee, I'm
23   going outside to lay on the lawn.'
24   'There's thousands of other worms out there,' Griselda murmured,
25   unearthing an apple on the table among some envelope's and the television
26   license.
27   'Who's is this?' he demanded, taking a deep bite from it. 'You and me
28   will talk later,' he glowered.
29   Turning to leave, the niblick swung round and struck the cup in
30   Griseldas hand.
31   'Help,' she cried, as the hot coffee scalded her lip.

(for the corrected version, turn the page)

Index

That's better!

So how did you get on with that dastardly test on the previous page? Here's our amended version, the figures in bold type referring to the line numbers.

1 Between you and me (object). **2** children's (apostrophe-s after the plural form). It's (It has). affected (influenced). **3** fine spring (no comma needed). morning. The garden (two sentences, requiring full stop and capital letter). its (possessive). **4** Tara and I.
5 uninterested. practise (verb). **6** fewer. **7** - a niblick - (two dashes needed as brackets).
9 imply (not infer). deny (not refute). **10** her story, Griselda (unattached participle: the climax hadn't started the story!). **13** their (possessive). its/its or their/their (consistently singular or plural). **14** matters to you (no question mark, because it's a statement).
15 would have. **16** theirs. For whom (object). They're (They are). principal (chief).
17 Try to. **18** won nearly all (nearly should qualify 'all', not 'won'). persisted, starting (comma needed). **19** everyone was. might have won (there's no doubt that they didn't win them all). **20** advice (noun). **22** past (verb). Your (possessive). **23** lie (present tense).
24 There are thousands (*there's* means *there is*, singular). **25** envelopes (plain plural).
26 licence (noun). **27** Whose (not *Who is*). You and I (subject). **29** to leave, he swung (unattached participle). **30** Griselda's (possessive). **31** 'Help!' (exclamation mark required).

30